Dear Parents and Educators,

Welcome to Penguin Young Readers! As parents and educators, you know that each child develops at his or her own pace—in terms of speech, critical thinking, and, of course, reading. Penguin Young Readers recognizes this fact. As a result, each Penguin Young Readers book is assigned a traditional easy-to-read level (1–4) as well as a Guided Reading Level (A–P). Both of these systems will help you choose the right book for your child. Please refer to the back of each book for specific leveling information. Penguin Young Readers features esteemed authors and illustrators, stories about favorite characters, fascinating nonfiction, and more!

Life in the Amazon Rainforest

LEVEL **4**

GUIDED READING LEVEL **O**

This book is perfect for a **Fluent Reader** who:
- can read the text quickly with minimal effort;
- has good comprehension skills;
- can self-correct (can recognize when something doesn't sound right); and
- can read aloud smoothly and with expression.

Here are some **activities** you can do during and after reading this book:
- Comprehension: After reading the book, answer the following questions:
  - How many layers have scientists divided the Amazon rainforest into? List the name of each layer.
  - How long can a capybara hold its breath underwater?
  - What are some ways you can help save the rainforest?
- Using a Glossary: A glossary, like a dictionary, tells you what words mean. Look at the words and their definitions in the glossary at the back of this book. Then write an original sentence for each word.

Remember, sharing the love of reading with a child is the best gift you can give!

—Sarah Fabiny, Editorial Director
  Penguin Young Readers program

*Penguin Young Readers are leveled by independent reviewers applying the standards developed by Irene Fountas and Gay Su Pinnell in *Matching Books to Readers: Using Leveled Books in Guided Reading*, Heinemann, 1999.

For Dylan R. Clarke, my capable research
assistant, enthusiastic first reader, and
favorite boy in the whole wide world!—GLC

PENGUIN YOUNG READERS
An Imprint of Penguin Random House LLC

Adapted from *What's Up in the Amazon Rainforest* by Ginjer L. Clarke, published in 2015 by
Grosset & Dunlap, an imprint of Penguin Random House LLC. Text copyright © 2018 by Ginjer L. Clarke.
All rights reserved. Published by Penguin Young Readers, an imprint of Penguin Random House LLC,
345 Hudson Street, New York, New York 10014. Manufactured in China.

Library of Congress Cataloging-in-Publication Data is available.

ISBN 9781524784874 (pbk)   10 9 8 7 6 5 4 3
ISBN 9781524784881 (hc)   10 9 8 7 6 5 4 3 2 1

PENGUIN YOUNG READERS

LEVEL

FLUENT
READER

4

LIFE IN THE
AMAZON RAINFOREST

by Ginjer L. Clarke

Penguin Young Readers
An Imprint of Penguin Random House

Introduction

A noisy animal lets out its whooping call. All around, you smell sweet flowers, stinky fruit, and animal poop.

Yikes! A huge snake slithers by. Rainbow-colored birds soar through the trees.

Where are you? The Amazon rainforest! This tropical rainforest in South America is one of the most amazing **habitats** on the planet.

What Is the Amazon Rainforest?

The continent of South America is very wide at the top and narrow at the bottom. At the wide part is the Amazon rainforest, which is almost as big as the United States, not including Alaska and Hawaii. Most of the rainforest is in Brazil.

Of all rainforests, the Amazon is the largest. More **species** of animals and plants live there than in any other habitat.

Animals and plants thrive in the Amazon rainforest because it is hot and sunny all the time—and also very wet.

Flash! Crash! Thunderstorms in the Amazon can be 40 times more powerful than storms in the United States.

With lots of sunshine and rain, the trees grow tall and provide a home and food for millions of animals.

Scientists have divided the Amazon rainforest into five main layers.

The Amazon River gives water, food, and shelter to many species.

The forest floor is the bottom of the rainforest. It is dark, hot, and quiet.

The understory is the bushes and small trees that grow below the tall trees.

The canopy (say: KAN-uh-pee) is the rainforest's roof, made of tall trees.

The emergent (say: e-MUR-junt) trees poke through, or emerge from, the canopy.

The Amazon River

The mighty Amazon River is about 4,000 miles long. It flows across South America from the Pacific Ocean to the Atlantic Ocean. It is considered the longest river in the world, including its **tributaries**.

It is also the widest river. It can swell to about 30 miles wide and 100 feet deep! When this happens, the forests and villages around the river fill up with water, too.

Splash! A pink dolphin pops out of the flooded river.

The Amazon river dolphin grabs a catfish with its long, thin beak. *Crush!* It breaks the fish into smaller bites with its strong, cone-shaped teeth.

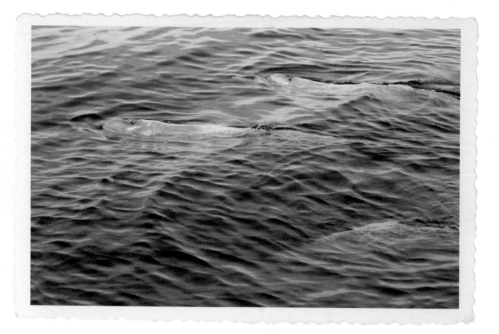

It is difficult for the river dolphin to see as it swims underwater. It has very small eyes, and the water is dark and murky. So the river dolphin uses **echolocation** to travel through the flooded forest.

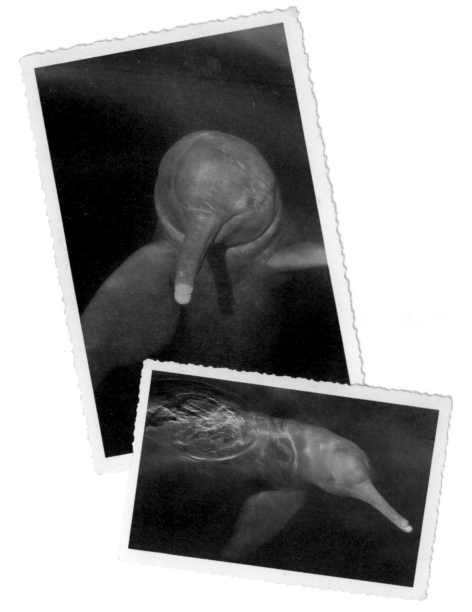

Another animal swimming in the river is the capybara (say: cap-ee-BAR-uh).

The capybara is the largest rodent in the world. It is the size of a large dog.

Capybaras live in family groups, with one male capybara as the leader. *Bark!* The leader warns the group that a caiman, a type of alligator, is nearing.

The capybaras dive underwater to
hide. They can hold their breath for up
to five minutes.
Then they poke
their heads out
and see that
the caiman has
swum away. That
was close!

The caiman rests quietly in the river, with only its eyes above water. *Snap!* The caiman snatches a fish. It eats almost any prey that comes near its powerful jaws.

Suddenly, a huge green anaconda grabs the caiman with its teeth. The anaconda pulls its prey into the water—and gives it a death hug!

An anaconda is a constrictor, which means it squeezes its prey to death. *Gulp!* The anaconda opens its jaws wide and swallows the caiman whole.

The Rainforest Floor

Hiding in the dark is the jaguar, the largest cat in South America and the top predator of the rainforest floor. The jaguar does not have any enemies besides humans. But the jaguar is **endangered** because people hunt it for its beautiful fur.

The jaguar's spotted coat helps it hide in the low branches of trees to surprise its prey. *Pounce!* The jaguar spots a tapir and jumps down to attack. The tapir dives into the river to escape.

The tapir (say: TAY-per) is a fast swimmer for its size. It is the largest land animal in the Amazon. It looks like a big, fuzzy pig with a short elephant trunk, but it is related to the rhinoceros.

The tapir moves its trunk along the ground, looking for food. It is an herbivore, so it eats only plants and fruit. It has to eat a lot to get energy for its big body.

Like the tapir, the giant anteater sniffs out food with its snout. It finds ants underground using its excellent sense of smell. It tears an opening into a nest of ants with its sharp front claws. *Lick! Flick!* It grabs the ants with its giant tongue and gulps them down.

Ants attacking a spider

The army ants fight back, stinging the anteater. They are also fierce predators. They march in lines of up to one million ants, feasting on everything in their path.

The Understory

The chicken-size hoatzin (say: wat-SEEN) is one of many birds that eat plants in the understory. *Ewww!* What is that smell? The hoatzin is nicknamed the "stinkbird" because it smells like cow poop.

The hoatzin's stink usually keeps away predators, but its chick does not smell, so it is in danger.

An emerald tree boa coils around a branch. It uses pits near its mouth to sense the heat of a hoatzin chick. The boa stretches to grab the baby bird. *Squeeze!* It constricts the chick to stop it from breathing and eats it—all in one bite.

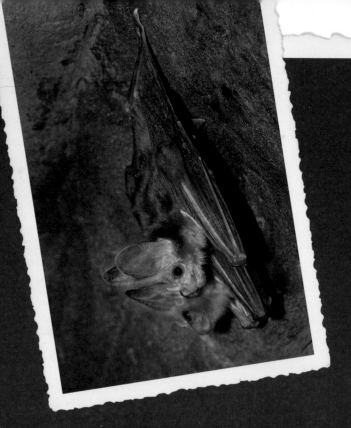

Another creature is hiding in the trees waiting to attack—the vampire bat. It has only one food source—blood! *Swoop!* A vampire bat flies down from the trees. It climbs onto a sleeping tapir, using sharp claws on the ends of its wings to grab the animal's slippery hair.

The bat pierces the tapir's skin with its sharp fangs. It drinks an ounce of blood in about 30 minutes. This meal fills up the bat for the night.

The ocelot (say: OS-uh-lot) is a
nocturnal cat that hunts at night. Its
keen ears hear a bat's wings flapping.
Leap! It jumps into the air and catches
the bat with its pointed front teeth.
Rip! The ocelot tears the bat
into pieces and swallows
them whole.

The Canopy

Wheee! The black spider monkey swings on a vine dangling from a tall tree. It leaps, flips, and runs through the treetops.

The black spider
monkey has a big brain
for its body size. It is
smart and sometimes
sneaky. *Crash!* It breaks
off a heavy branch and
drops it onto a group
of small monkeys called
marmosets. It is warning
them to keep away.

The pygmy marmoset is the world's smallest monkey. It could fit in the palm of your hand!

Still, pygmy marmosets are fierce. To fight off a spider monkey, the marmosets turn around and stick their bottoms in the monkey's face. *Shriek!* They yell at the monkey with high-pitched sounds that humans cannot hear.

The three-toed sloth hangs around quietly during all this action. The sloth is the slowest mammal on Earth. It can take a sloth more than an hour to creep 10 feet along a tree branch!

A sloth eats mostly
leaves. This diet does not give it
much energy, so it sleeps
up to 20 hours per day.
A sloth only comes down
to the ground to go to
the bathroom—about
once a week!

The Emergent Trees

Plants called bromeliads (say: bro-MILL-ee-adz) grow on the tall emergent trees. Tiny tree frogs live their whole lives in these plants.

The poison dart frog is only one inch long, but it is deadly! Its bright colors warn predators that it tastes bad and is poisonous. Anything that eats it, or even licks it, will die almost instantly.

This frog got its name because some rainforest people use the frog's poison on their blowgun darts to hunt animals for food.

Another colorful creature lands in the treetops. It is a scarlet macaw! Macaws are the largest parrots in the world. And they're noisy, too.

Squawk! This male macaw calls out to a female. She returns his call, and he soars over to meet her. They glide above the trees to find their favorite fruit. Macaws can eat fruits that are poisonous to other animals. They also eat dirt from the riverbank, which may help their stomachs break down these fruits.

The only rainforest animal noisier than the macaw is the red howler monkey. The calls of male howler monkeys can be heard up to three miles away. *Whoop!* A male howler monkey roars to alert his troop of danger.

A harpy eagle swoops in! It is the most feared predator in the treetops. *Zoom!* It snatches a howler monkey out of a tree with its strong talons. It flies with the monkey back to its nest and gobbles up its catch.

Saving the Amazon Rainforest

Rainforest trees are important to a healthy planet. They take carbon dioxide, a gas that is dangerous in large amounts, out of the **atmosphere**. They also help slow down **global warming** by giving off oxygen, which we need to breathe.

We also get many delicious foods, useful products, and helpful medicines from the rainforest, but we are not taking care of this important habitat.

Sadly, the rainforest is shrinking fast. Many trees are cut down to make furniture and paper products. Other parts of the forest are burned to create farms. The Amazon is in danger!

What can *you* do to help save the rainforest? Buying products that are marked as Fair Trade is a good start. This supports companies that provide these goods without destroying more of the rainforest. Practicing the three Rs— Reduce, Reuse, Recycle—is also very helpful to

keep more trees from being cut down.

The choices we make now will shape the future of this rainforest. What will you do to make a difference for our wild, wonderful world?

Glossary

atmosphere: the ring of gases surrounding Earth or another planet

echolocation: the location of objects by reflected sound, used by animals such as dolphins and bats

endangered: animals and places that are at risk of extinction, or dying out forever

global warming: an increase in Earth's temperature caused by gases getting trapped in the atmosphere

habitat: the place where animals, plants, and people are adapted to live

nocturnal: animals that hunt at night and sleep during the day

species: a group of living things with similar traits

tributaries: smaller rivers and streams that flow into a larger river